# desserts & drinks

# desserts
# & drinks
## from around the world

**ni**

Chunky Cook Books series
Desserts & Drinks from around the world

First published in the UK in 2004 by
New Internationalist™ Publications Ltd
55 Rectory Road
Oxford OX4 1BW, UK.
**www.newint.org**
New Internationalist is a registered trade mark.

Cover image: © Claude Sauvageot

Food photography: Caroline Svensson, copyright © Kam & Co, Denmark
Email: studiet@kam.dk
Copyright © all other photographs: individual photographers/agencies.

Design by Alan Hughes/New Internationalist.

Printed in Italy by Amadeus.

Printed on recycled paper.

British Library Cataloguing-in-Publication Data.
A catalogue record for this book is available from the British Library.

Library of Congress Cataloguing-in-Publication Data.
A catalogue for this book is available from the Library of Congress.

ISBN 1 904456 16 2

# contents

Introduction                        6

Africa                              8

Asia                               36

Latin America & Caribbean          90

Middle East & North Africa        132

Food Facts                        166

Fair Trade Food                   170

Index                             172

About the NI                      175

# introduction

**Almond pastries, hot gingerbreads**, banana fritters, sweet milk desserts, not to mention fresh lime juice and cool rum cocktails – this collection includes a wealth of wonderful desserts and drinks for you to try.

Have a look through and see the enticing selection of dishes and drinks, many captured by the studio of award-winning Danish photographer Peter Kam. These recipes are easy to prepare and taste even better with fair trade organic goods.

Of course, most of the recipes use a sweetener, and that commonly is refined sugar or sucrose. And sugar, even fairly traded and organic, is a mixed blessing. Many of us succumb to the desire for something sweet at some point, even if we generally prefer savory tastes. There is something about sugar in its many guises that draws us in, that comforts and reassures us. It gives us energy, of course. A boost to our blood-sugar level really does make us high and raring to go – for a while. Like alcohol, sugar seems to give us a lift (although alcohol is in fact a depressant; it works first to dampen anxieties and inhibitions so that we feel lifted). In chocolate, the combination of sugar and cocoa is irresistible for many people.

Sugar has a dirty history, bound up with the slave trade. In the 16th century Europeans began taking Africans as slaves across the Atlantic to work on sugar plantations. In this 'triangular trade', sugar and other commodities were brought from the New

World to Europe; then on the final leg, manufactured goods such as firearms and cloth were transported to Africa. All the more galling then is the fact that, nutritionally, humans do not need sugar, and certainly not refined sugar. Many foods contain their own sweetness (fructose or lactose) and that is sufficient. Refined sugar just piles on calories devoid of nutrients, and also piles up profits for big companies who control the trade today.

The biggest sugar producer is India, with 24,000 tons annually, but most of that is consumed in the subcontinent. Brazil is the largest exporter, followed by Australia, Thailand and Cuba.

Bananas also feature in several of the recipes in this book. The bananas that are traded on the world markets today are largely grown in huge plantations, sometimes in working conditions that closely resemble slavery.

But things are gradually changing. Small growers in the Dominican Republic, for example, are exporting bananas that are not only fairly traded but also organic. On the sugar front, non-refined sugars such as Demerara are available as fair trade and organic items.

It is worth making the effort to find and buy fair trade or organic ingredients. Not only will the recipes in this book taste even more delicious, but you will be making a positive contribution to ethical trading and global justice. ∎

africa

# peanut bread

serves **8-12**

**4 tablespoons peanuts,
finely chopped or minced**

**3 cups / 375 g flour**

**4 teaspoons
baking powder**

**2 tablespoons sugar**

**salt**

**1 egg**

**1½ cups / 350 ml milk**

*Heat oven to
350°F/180°C/Gas 4*

1 Using a mixing bowl, first sieve the flour, baking powder, sugar and salt into it.

2 Crack the egg into another bowl, beat it and then stir in the milk. Now pour this into the dry ingredients and mix together.

3 When this is done, add the peanuts and blend them into the mixture. Spoon the bread into a greased tin and leave it to stand for 20 minutes.

4 After that, put the bread into the oven and bake for about 1 hour. Then turn it out of the tin and let it cool on a wire tray. Serve with savory dishes, or else with jelly/jam or syrup.

# soybean scones

serves **8-12**

1 cup / 125 g soy flour

3³/₄ cups / 450 g wheat flour

salt

1 egg

2 tablespoons sugar

a little milk or water

2 tablespoons oil

**1** Begin by mixing the soy and wheat flours together with the salt in a bowl.

**2** Then, in a separate bowl, beat the egg and sugar together and stir this into the flour, adding enough milk or water to make a stiff dough.

**3** Heat the oil in a heavy pan and carefully put in spoonfuls of the mixture. Let these cook on both sides for about 10 minutes until done. Repeat until all the mixture is used up, and serve hot or cold with main dishes or with jelly/jam.

# banana bread

serves **6**

**1<sup>3</sup>/<sub>4</sub> cups / 225 g flour**

**1 teaspoon bicarbonate of soda**

**1 teaspoon baking powder**

**2 tablespoons margarine**

**<sup>1</sup>/<sub>3</sub> cup / 75 g sugar**

**2 eggs, beaten**

**3 ripe bananas, mashed**

**salt**

*Heat oven to 350°F/180°C/Gas 4*

**1** Sift the flour together with the bicarbonate of soda, baking powder and a little salt into a bowl.

**2** In another bowl, cream the margarine with the sugar and then add the beaten eggs, a little at a time. If the mixture curdles, put in some of the flour and mix well.

**3** The mashed bananas and the flour can go in now; stir well.

**4** Next, grease a loaf tin and spoon in the mixture. Bake for about 1 hour or until done – test by piercing with a kebab skewer or knitting needle. It should come out clean.

**5** Remove the bread from the oven but leave it to stand in the tin for 15 minutes. Then turn it out to cool on a rack. If possible, leave until the next day before serving, cut into slices spread with margarine if liked.

# docono

serves **2-4**

semolina dessert

**3 tablespoons semolina**

**1-2 tablespoons sugar**

**2¹/₂ cups / 590 ml milk**

**¹/₂ teaspoon vanilla essence**

**¹/₂ teaspoon cinnamon**

**2 bananas, sliced**

**1** Place the semolina in a mixing bowl together with the sugar and pour in enough cold milk to make a paste.

**2** Now put the rest of the milk on to boil. When it reaches boiling point, pour it into the semolina paste, a little at a time, stirring constantly so that the mixture is smooth.

**3** Return this now to the saucepan and bring it to the boil, stirring frequently to prevent catching.

**4** Let the semolina simmer for 5-10 minutes and then take it from the heat and stir in the vanilla essence, cinnamon and sliced bananas. Serve at once, or leave it to cool.

serves **4-6**

# corn/maize meal loaf

²/₃ cup / 100 g self-raising maize/corn meal (or plain, but then add 4 teaspoons baking powder)

1 cup / 125 g wheat flour

salt

2 tablespoons sugar or to taste

1 egg, beaten

2 tablespoons / 25 g margarine, melted

¹/₂ cup / 120 ml milk

**1** First, shake the flours, baking powder (if used), salt and sugar into a bowl.

**2** Then add the beaten egg, melted margarine and enough milk to make a fairly stiff mixture.

**3** Mix well together and then spoon it into a greased loaf or cake tin. Spread the mixture evenly and then cook the bread for about 20-30 minutes. After this, leave it to cool a while before serving. You can eat the bread with margarine and jelly/jam or honey or on its own to accompany savory meals.

*Heat oven to 350°F/180°C/Gas 4*

# paw-paw/ papaya & mango fool

serves **4**

**1 cup / 200 g paw-paw/papaya, mashed**

**1 cup / 200 g mango, mashed**

**2 tablespoons lemon juice**

**sugar to taste**

**1/2 cup / 120 ml double or whipping cream**

1 Begin by putting the mashed or puréed fruits in a bowl. Then stir in the lemon juice and add sugar as required, mixing everything well so that the sugar dissolves.

2 Now whip the cream in a large basin until it is thick and firm. Gently fold in the fruit mixture. Then turn the fool into a serving dish and place in the fridge to chill.

# fruit salad

serves **6**

**2¹/₂ cups / 450 g paw-paw/papaya***

**1 small pineapple**

**2 large mangoes**

**3 pears or apples**

**3 bananas**

**4 passion fruits/ grenadillos⁺**

**juice of 3 oranges**

*If using canned fruit, drain off the liquid. The quantities you end up with may be different from the amounts given in the recipe but as long as you have a good mix of fruit, the actual quantities do not matter too much.

⁺optional ingredient

1 First peel and slice or cube all the fruit except the passion fruits.

2 After this, put the fruit into a large bowl and mix well. Now cut the passion fruits in half and scoop the pulp into the bowl, add the orange juice and mix everything round. Chill in the fridge before serving.

# grenadillo* dessert

serves **6-8**

**12 passion fruits/grenadillos**

**1 cup / 240 ml water**

**sugar to taste**

**juice of 2 oranges**

**1 tablespoon gelatine, soaked in a little cold water or vegetarian thickened**

**2 eggs, separated**

*passion fruit

**1** Cut the passion fruits in half and scoop out the pulp and seeds into a pan. Add the water and bring to the boil. Then turn down the heat and simmer for 1 minute.

**2** When this is done, sieve the mixture into a bowl. Add the sugar, orange juice and soaked gelatine.

**3** Now pour the mixture into a pan and heat it gently, stirring until the gelatine is completely dissolved.

**4** Allow the mixture to cool. When it is lukewarm, beat the egg yolks lightly and stir them in. Set aside until the mixture begins to set.

**5** At this point, whisk the egg whites until they are stiff and fold them in. Put the dessert into a dish and refrigerate until completely set. Serve with cream or plain yogurt and wafer biscuits or shortbread.

# mbatata pudding

serves **2-4**

## sweet potato pudding

**2 sweet potatoes, chopped**

**2-3 teaspoons honey**

**1 tablespoon sherry or brandy***

**2 tablespoons margarine**

**1 egg, separated**

**rind and juice of an orange**

*optional ingredient

*Heat oven to 400°F/200°C/Gas 6*

**1** Place the sweet potatoes in a saucepan of boiling water and cook until they are soft, about 10 minutes. Drain and then put them into a bowl and mash them.

**2** Now add all the other ingredients, except the egg white, and mix them together.

**3** When this is done, whisk the egg white until it is stiff and then fold it into the mixture.

**4** Grease an ovenproof dish and spoon in the pudding. Bake until golden brown, about 45 minutes-1 hour.

MALI

# meni-meniyong

makes **6-8**

## sesame seed/simsim sticks

**1 cup / 100 g
sesame seeds**

**4 tablespoons / 50 g
margarine**

**1 cup / 350 ml honey or
1 cup / 175 g sugar or to
taste**

1 In a shallow pan, toast the sesame seeds without any oil until they begin to jump about and turn golden. Shake the pan so they do not stick or burn. When they are ready, put them to cool on one side.

2 Now, using a heavy pan, heat the margarine or oil and then add the sugar or honey. Stir continuously until it begins to caramelize.

3 Pour the sesame seeds into the warm mixture and stir thoroughly.

4 Transfer the mixture to a flat tin. As it cools, shape it into pieces either by cutting into squares or by rolling the mixture and then coating it with more sesame seeds if required.

# coconut cakes

makes **18**

**3 cups / 300 g freshly grated coconut or 4 cups / 300 g desiccated/shredded coconut**

**1¹/₂ cups / 150 g flour**

**3-4 tablespoons sugar**

**1 cup / 240 ml tablespoons water**

**¹/₂ teaspoon grated nutmeg**

**1** Mix together the coconut, flour and sugar.

**2** Gradually add the water, mixing to a stiff dough. Take up small amounts of the mixture and shape into balls. Place them on a greased baking tray, and press each one with a spoon to make them about ³/₄ inch/2 cm thick.

**3** Bake for 15-20 minutes or until golden brown. Cool, and sprinkle with additional nutmeg before serving.

*Heat oven to 350°F/180°C/Gas 4*

# melktert

serves **4-6**

milk tart

½ pound / 225 g frozen pastry, thawed

2 eggs, separated

2½ cups / 590 ml milk

2½ tablespoons cornstarch/cornflour

2 tablespoons sugar

piece of cinnamon

½ teaspoon cinnamon powder

*Heat oven to 425°F/220°C/Gas 7*

**1** Roll out the pastry extremely thinly and then line an 8 inch/20 cm pie dish with it. Cut a circle of waxed/greaseproof paper, place this on the pastry and weight it with some dried beans. Bake the pastry-case for 8-10 minutes and then remove it from the oven and set aside.

**2** Turn down the oven to 325°F/160°C/Gas 3.

**3** Separate the eggs and beat the yolks with the sugar.

**4** Spoon the cornstarch/cornflour into a small bowl and add a little of the milk to make a smooth paste. Set the rest of the milk on to boil, and toss in the stick of cinnamon.

**5** When the milk is at boiling point, pour some back into the cornstarch/cornflour mixture and blend well. Then return this to the saucepan containing the milk.

**6** Bring to the boil gently, stirring all the time as it thickens. When it is creamy, remove from the heat and set aside to cool a little, stirring from time to time to prevent skin forming. Take out the piece of cinnamon.

**7** When the milk is cool, add the beaten yolk and sugar mixture. Now whisk the egg whites until they are stiff and then fold these in. Stir everything together so that it mingles and then spoon it into the waiting pie case.

**8** Sprinkle a little cinnamon powder and sugar if liked on the top and bake the pie for 1 hour or until set – firm to the touch and not wobbly when you gently shake the dish. Serve cool or cold.

# SUDAN

# ful-sudani

makes **10-12**

peanut macaroons

**1 cup / 125 g unsalted peanuts**

**1 egg white**

**pinch of salt**

**³/₄ cup / 130 g sugar**

**¹/₂ teaspoon vanilla, almond or lemon flavoring**

**waxed/greaseproof paper**

*Heat oven to 350°F/180°C/Gas 4*

**1** Brown the peanuts under the grill, shaking them and turning frequently so that they do not burn. Then chop or grind them coarsely.

**2** Whisk the egg white with a pinch of salt until stiff, and then fold in the sugar and vanilla flavoring and whisk again. Add the peanuts.

**3** Put some waxed/greaseproof paper on a baking tray and grease it lightly.

**4** Using a teaspoon, put small heaps of the nut mixture onto the baking tray and cook for about 20-25 minutes until the macaroons are golden.

asia

# mal pua

makes about **15** small pancakes

## coconut pancakes

**1 cup / 75 g dried/desiccated coconut**

**1 cup / 110 g rice flour or wheat flour**

**1 cup / 240 ml milk**

**1-2 tablespoons sugar**

**seeds from 1 cardamom pod, crushed**

**oil**

**FOR THE SYRUP***

**1 cup / 240 ml water**

**1 cup / 225 g sugar**

*optional

1 In a bowl, mix the coconut, flour and milk together to make a runny paste, if necessary adding a drop more milk. Then sprinkle in the sugar and cardamom seeds and stir well.

2 Heat enough oil for deep frying in a wok (about 2 inches/5 cms) and when it is very hot, take a spoonful of the mixture and slide it into the oil. It will quickly form a small pancake. Deep-fry on both sides to a golden brown.

3 Remove the pancake from the wok and drain on kitchen paper. Keep warm while you cook the rest. Eat as they are, or with honey, or syrup, see below.

4 For the syrup, boil the water and then stir in the sugar. Boil vigorously for 10-20 minutes until the mixture transforms into syrup. Let it cool a bit and then deftly dip in the pancakes before eating at once.

# semolina cake

serves **6-8**

**<sup>3</sup>/<sub>4</sub> cup / 110 g semolina**

**<sup>1</sup>/<sub>2</sub> tablespoon sesame seeds**

**<sup>1</sup>/<sub>4</sub> cup / 30 g almond slivers**

**2<sup>1</sup>/<sub>2</sub> cups / 590 ml milk**

**<sup>1</sup>/<sub>2</sub> cup / 120 ml thick coconut cream\***

**1 egg**

**<sup>1</sup>/<sub>2</sub> cup / 85 g sugar**

**seeds from 1 cardamom pod, crushed**

\*To make this, melt <sup>1</sup>/<sub>2</sub> cup/50 g creamed coconut in 1 cup/120 ml hot water

*Heat oven to 350°F/180°C/Gas 4*

**1** First, toast the sesame seeds and almond slivers separately, either under the broiler/grill or in a pan with a drop of oil until they begin to turn golden.

**2** Now put the semolina into another pan. Cook and dry over a moderate heat until it turns light golden brown, stirring and shaking frequently to prevent burning. Then remove it from the heat to cool.

**3** Pour the milk and coconut cream into a saucepan and heat them gently, stirring to blend them. Remove from heat.

**4** When this is done, beat the egg and sugar together in a bowl with a wooden spoon until the mixture becomes light and smooth. Stir in the crushed cardamom seeds and almonds.

**5** After this, pour the milk and coconut cream mixture into the pan containing the cooled semolina. Cook gently over a low heat, stirring constantly to prevent burning and lumps forming, until it is very thick. Remove from the heat and then stir in the egg and sugar mixture.

**6** Now place the cake in a greased 6 inch/15 cm square cake tin and smooth the top. Sprinkle on the sesame seeds, cover with foil and cook in a larger tin of hot water in the oven for about 1 hour. Leave to cool completely and then cut into pieces. Store the cake in the fridge.

# semolina dessert

serves **4**

1 cup / 150 g semolina

2 tablespoons coconut milk

1-2 tablespoons sugar

seeds of 1 cardamom pod, crushed

2 tablespoons dried/desiccated coconut

$2^1/_2$ cups / 590 ml water or milk, or a mixture of the two

oil

**1** Start by heating the oil in a wok or large pan and then put in the semolina. Stir it briskly for a few minutes until it begins to brown.

**2** Reduce the heat now and pour in the coconut milk, mixing well, and continue to cook for 3-4 minutes.

**3** At this point, put in the sugar and cardamom and stir again. Pour in the water and/or milk, adding more of these if needed to obtain the desired consistency. Serve hot with the desiccated coconut sprinkled on top.

# peanut & sesame crunch

makes **24-30** pieces

2 cups / 250 g unsalted roasted peanuts

$^{1}/_{2}$ cup / 50 g sesame seeds

2 cups / 350 g sugar

$^{1}/_{3}$ cup / 80 ml white wine vinegar

4 teaspoons water

**1** First of all, toast the sesame seeds. To do this, put a heavy pan on the cooker without any oil or fat. Heat it and then put the seeds in and shake them around as they brown; they will jump too. You can also brown them in the broiler/grill for a few minutes if you prefer.

**2** Then mix the sugar, vinegar and water in a pan over a low heat, stirring until the sugar dissolves.

**3** Now bring the mixture to the boil and let it cook without stirring until it is golden and reaches 295° to 300°F/146° to 149°C – 'hard-crack' stage. If you have no candy thermometer, test for this by taking a teaspoon and dipping it into the mixture. Then allow the syrup to drop into a sauce of cold water. It should harden and snap with a clean break if it is ready. If it does not, continue to boil and test it again.

**3** Grease a 11 x 7 inch/28 x 18 cm baking tray. Sprinkle half of the sesame seeds and all the peanuts evenly over the bottom.

**4** Pour the sugar mixture over the nuts and seeds and then sprinkle on the remaining sesame seeds. Allow it to cool slightly and cut into small pieces. Leave it in the baking tray to cool and harden completely.

# hsing jen cha

serves **4**

## almond dessert

**³/₄ cup / 200 g pudding rice**

**³/₄ cup / 100 g almonds**

**2¹/₂ cups / 590 ml water**

**4-6 tablespoons sugar**

**1 teaspoon almond essence or seeds of 1 cardamom pod, crushed**

**a few shelled pistachios or whole unskinned almonds**

**1** Drain the rice and almonds and grind them in a blender. Then put the mixture into a heavy pan and pour in the water; bring to the boil.

**2** Cook very gently for 30 minutes, stirring frequently.

**3** When the rice is ready, add the sugar and the almond essence and stir well until the sugar dissolves and the flavors have fused. Decorate with pistachios or whole, unskinned almonds.

# banana fudge

makes **12**

**1 large banana**

**seeds from 3 cardamom pods, crushed**

**2 tablespoons / 25 g margarine**

**1/4 cup / 50 g semolina**

**1/4 cup / 50 g ground almonds**

**1/3 cup / 60 g sugar**

**1-2 teaspoons water**

**1** To begin, put the banana into a bowl and mash it with a fork. Add the crushed cardamom seeds and mix well.

**2** Now melt the margarine in a pan and gently cook the semolina until it turns golden. When this is ready, add the banana mixture, ground almonds, sugar and a little water, taking care that it does not become too wet.

**3** Bring to the boil and cook, stirring constantly, until the mixture comes away from the sides of the pan.

**4** Spoon it into a shallow greased tin and let it cool a little. Then put it into the fridge to set. Cut into small pieces or roll into balls to serve.

# coconut sweet

makes **15** pieces

$^3/_4$ cup / 180 ml
evaporated milk

$^1/_2$ cup / 85 g sugar

$1^1/_4$ cups / 100 g
desiccated coconut

1 First of all, pour the evaporated milk into a pan and add the sugar. Heat gently, stirring from time to time. When it boils, turn down the heat and simmer until the milk has reduced by half.

2 Now put in the coconut and continue stirring until the mixture sticks together in a ball. Then remove it from the pan and transfer it to a greased shallow dish or toffee tray. Spread it evenly, using the back of a spoon.

3 Leave the mixture to cool and then cut it into pieces.

# kulfi

serves **4-6**

## ice-cream with pistachio nuts

**2 quarts / 2 liters milk**

**10 whole cardamom pods**

**4-5 tablespoons sugar**

**1 cup / 125 g almonds,
chopped**

**$1/2$ cup / 60 g shelled,
unsalted pistachio nuts***

*If you cannot find unsalted
pistachios, use salted ones but
wash and dry them after shelling.

**1** To start, bring the milk to the boil in a heavy pan. As it begins to rise, turn down the heat and let it simmer without boiling over.

**2** Add the cardamom pods now and continue to simmer the milk until it has reduced to one-third its original quantity. Stir frequently.

**3** When this is done, take out the cardamoms. Then add the sugar and almonds and simmer again for 2-3 minutes.

**4** Now remove the milk from the heat and pour it into a bowl. Leave it to cool.

**5** After this, add half the pistachios. Cover the bowl with foil and put it in the freezer, taking it out and stirring every 15 minutes to prevent crystals forming.

**6** When it is almost frozen, transfer the kulfi to a serving dish that has been cooled in the freezer, sprinkle the remaining pistachios on top and put it back in the freezer to harden before serving.

INDIA

# lassi

serves **4**

## yogurt drink

2 small cartons plain
yogurt

2$^{1}/_{2}$ cups / 590 ml cold
water

juice of $^{1}/_{2}$ lemon

2 teaspoons sugar*

*a little salt can be used to flavor
instead of sugar

1 Simply whisk or liquidize all ingredients until frothy and pour into glasses.

# tea with cardamom

serves **2-4**

seeds from 6 cardamom
pods, crushed

4 cups / 1 liter water

1 teaspoon tea leaves

3 tablespoons sugar

$2^1/_2$ cups / 590 ml milk

**1** To make the tea, boil the water with the cardamom seeds for 5 minutes, using a saucepan.

**2** After this, add the tea leaves and continue to cook for a few minutes.

**3** Now put in the sugar and cook, stirring until it dissolves. Finally, pour in the milk, bring to the boil again and simmer for 10-15 minutes before serving.

# aam ras

serves **4**

## mango dessert

**5 cups / 750 g mango pulp**

**1 cup / 220 ml single cream**

**seeds of 3 green cardamom pods, crushed**

**a few strands of saffron infused in a little warm milk\***

**sugar to taste**

\*optional ingredient

1 If using fresh mangoes, remove the skin and slice the fruit into a bowl. Then cut it into very small pieces or put it into a blender.

2 Put the mango pulp, cream, cardamom seeds and saffron if using into a blender and whizz for a few seconds to combine, or mix the ingredients well in a bowl with hand beater or whisk. Chill before serving.

# christmas cakes

makes **2** cakes

**2 cups / 225 g mixed peel**

**2 cups / 225 g currants**

**2 cups / 225 g raisins or sultanas**

**2 cups / 250 g almonds or cashew nuts (or mixed half and half)**

**1/2 cup / 50 g glacé cherries**

**1 teaspoon ground mixed spice**

**1/2 cup / 50 g preserved ginger, finely chopped**

**1/4 cup / 60 ml rum or brandy**

**1/2 pound / 225 g semolina**

**1/2 cup / 60 g self-raising flour**

**1 1/2 cups / 350 g sugar**

**1/2 pound / 225 g margarine**

**6 eggs, separated**

**1/4 cup / 60 ml milk**

**1/4 teaspoon salt**

*Heat oven to 350°F/180°C/Gas 4*

**1** Chop the nuts and dried fruit and put them into a container with a lid and pour the rum or brandy on top. Leave to soak for a week.

**2** When ready to make the cake, take a large bowl and cream the margarine with 1 cup/225 g of the sugar to produce a smooth consistency.

**3** Beat the egg yolks now and add them a little at a time, stirring well. Should the mixture begin to curdle, sift in some of the flour.

**4** The rest of the flour goes in now, together with the semolina. Then gradually add the mixture of soaked fruit and nuts and their liquor.

**5** Now whisk the egg whites to a stiff froth and fold them into the cake mixture.

**6** Next, spoon the remaining sugar into a saucepan. Place on the heat and cook, stirring all the time, until the sugar turns dark brown. When this is done, remove the pan from the heat and pour in the milk, stirring thoroughly. Put in the salt and then empty this mixture into the cake and stir well.

**7** Grease 2 x 8 inch/20 cm square cake tins, spoon in the mixture and bake in the middle of the oven for about $1^1/_2$ hours or until done. Leave cakes to cool in the tin for half an hour before turning out onto a rack or plate. Store in a tin or container with a tight-fitting lid.

# carrot halva serves 2-4

1/2 pound / 225 g
carrots, grated

4 cardamom pods

1 1/2 cups / 350 ml milk

2 tablespoons ghee
or margarine

2-4 tablespoons sugar

1 tablespoon sultanas

1 tablespoon unsalted
pistachio nuts, shelled
and lightly crushed or
use walnuts

1/2 cup / 110 g strained
yogurt or thick cream

**1** Place the grated carrots with the cardamom pods into a heavy saucepan and pour in the milk.

**2** Bring to the boil and then reduce the heat and cook, stirring from time to time, until virtually all the liquid has evaporated – this will take $^1/_2$ hour or more.

**3** Now warm the margarine or ghee in a pan and put in the carrot mixture. Stir and fry for 10-15 minutes until the carrots lose their wet milkiness and turn a rich reddish color.

**4** At this point, sprinkle in the sugar, sultanas and pistachios or walnuts. Stir-fry for a further 2 minutes and serve with yogurt or cream.

# fruit salad

serves **4-6**

**1 large can or medium fresh papaya/paw-paw**

**2 bananas**

**1 wedge watermelon**

**1 mango**

**1 zalak, 4 lychees or 1 apple**

**4 slices pineapple**

**juice of 1 lime/lemon**

**1 tablespoon brown sugar**

**dash of rum***

**cream/coconut milk***

*optional ingredients

NOTE: If using fresh papaya/paw-paw you can serve the salad in the halves of the fruit itself. Otherwise, a glass dish or other bowl will do.

**1** Cut the papaya/paw-paw into two halves, remove the seeds and carefully scoop out the flesh using a teaspoon so that the fruit curls into balls.

**2** Slice the other fruit into cubes and then arrange all the fruit either in the papaya/paw-paw skins or in a bowl. Sprinkle with lemon/lime juice, sugar and rum if desired.

**3** Serve with cream or coconut milk.

# skewered bananas with sauce

**8 small or 4 big bananas, peeled**

**4 tablespoons lemon or lime juice**

**1-2 tablespoons liquid honey**

**1 fresh red chili, chopped finely, or 1 teaspoon chili powder***

*The chili is what makes the dish distinctive, but if the idea does not appeal for a dessert, either omit that ingredient or serve the dish to accompany a savory meal such as curry.

**1** First, mix all the ingredients together in a bowl, except the bananas.

**2** Now thread the bananas lengthwise onto skewers and cook them over a charcoal barbecue or under the broiler/grill, turning constantly so they cook on all sides without burning.

**3** Now let them cool a little and take them from the skewers and dip them into the sauce as you eat them.

# tea with spices

For a **4-cup** teapot

**$^1/_2$ teaspoon green tea**

**3 cardamom pods**

**$^1/_2$ stick cinnamon**

**small slice fresh ginger**

**pinch of saffron***

**$^1/_2$ teaspoon ground almonds**

**water for a 4-cup teapot**

*optional ingredient

1 Bring all the ingredients to the boil and simmer for 2 minutes. Pour through a strainer.

# bubor chacha

serves **2-4**

## sweet potato dessert

½ pound / 225 g sweet potatoes, diced and boiled

1 cup / 240 ml coconut milk

½-1 tablespoon unrefined sugar

1 teaspoon kewra water*

½ cup / 120 ml water

pinch of cinnamon

salt

crushed ice

*optional ingredient, available from Asian stores.

1 Put the sugar into a pan and pour on the water; add the kewra water and simmer to dissolve the sugar. Then increase the heat and boil for 3-4 minutes or until the mixture begins to thicken.

2 Place the diced sweet potatoes in the sugar mixture and pour in the coconut milk. Sprinkle on a little salt and mix gently.

3 Put the crushed ice into small serving bowls and spoon the dessert over, garnishing with a little cinnamon.

# pisang pancakes

serves **4**

banana pancakes

**2 eggs**

**1 tablespoon sugar**

**1 cup / 125 g self-raising flour**

**1 tablespoon coconut cream**

**4-5 bananas, mashed**

**margarine**

**1** Begin by beating the eggs with the sugar. Then sift the flour and fold it into the eggs, a little at a time, alternating with pouring in the coconut cream.

**2** When that is done, scoop in the mashed bananas and mix well.

**3** Melt a little margarine in a frying pan and when it is hot pour in 2 tablespoons of the batter. Tilt the pan so that the pancake mix coats the bottom and cook until lightly brown. Then turn and cook the other side.

**4** Fold the pancake into a triangle and remove it from the pan; set aside to keep warm while you cook the others. Serve with wedges of lemon and banana slices.

# rum cake

serves **6**

**1¹/₂ cups / 180 g plain flour**

**4 eggs, beaten**

**³/₄ cup / 200 g sugar**

**¹/₄ pound / 110 g margarine**

**¹/₂ cup / 120 ml dark rum**

**1 tablespoon cornstarch/cornflour**

**¹/₄ teaspoon baking powder**

**grated zest and juice of 3 limes or 2 lemons**

*Heat oven to 350°F/180°C/Gas 4*

**1** First, grease an 8 inch/20 cm square cake tin. Sprinkle on some flour and then tap the tin to remove the excess.

**2** Sift the flour together with the cornstarch/cornflour and baking powder into a bowl.

**3** In another bowl, cream the margarine and sugar together. Then pour in the beaten eggs, a little at a time, and stir continuously. If the mixture curdles, shake in a little flour. Continue until all the eggs are incorporated.

**4** After this is done add the rum, grated rind and lime or lemon juice, adding more flour as necessary to make a smooth creamy mixture.

**5** Now fold in the remaining flour and stir well. Then pour the mixture into the cake tin, smooth the top, and cook in the middle of the oven for about 1 hour. When ready, remove from the oven and leave to cool in the tin.

# passion fruit cocktail

serves **2**

1/4 cup / 60 ml dark rum

1/2 cup / 120 ml passion
fruit or orange juice

2 teaspoons
coconut milk

4 fresh strawberries

dash of lime
or lemon juice

**1** Blend all the ingredients together
with crushed ice and serve.

# vattalappam serves **2-4**

spicy coconut dessert

2 large eggs

2 cups / 470 ml milk

3 tablespoons full-cream milk powder

1/2 cup / 50 g creamed coconut melted in 1/2 cup / 120 ml hot water

seeds from 3 cardamoms, crushed

1/2 teaspoon ground cinnamon

1/2 teaspoon grated nutmeg

1-2 tablespoons black molasses/treacle or to taste

1-2 tablespoons brown sugar or to taste

*Heat oven to 350°F/180°C/Gas 4*

**1** Start by beating the eggs lightly in a bowl.

**2** Then, using a fresh bowl, mix the milk with the milk powder, add the creamed coconut and then heat in a pan until it is just beginning to boil. Put in the spices and molasses and mix thoroughly.

**3** Pour the hot milk mixture into the bowl containing the beaten eggs, stir well, and transfer this to an oven-proof dish.

**4** Set the dish in a larger basin containing hot water and place in the oven for about 1 hour or until the pudding is set.

**5** Sprinkle on brown sugar and raise oven heat to crisp the top. Serve warm or cold.

# bananas in arrack

serves **2**

2 tablespoons margarine

2 ripe bananas, halved lengthwise

$^1/_3$ cup / 75 g brown sugar

seeds of 1 cardamom pod, crushed

juice of 1 lime

juice of 3 nectarines or 2 oranges

grated rind of 1 orange

$^1/_2$ teaspoon cinnamon

2 tablespoons arrack, brandy or red wine

**1** Melt half the margarine in a pan and lightly sauté the bananas until they are golden and semi-cooked. Then lift them out carefully and set aside.

**2** Now warm the rest of the margarine. Add the sugar and cardamom and stir continuously. When the sugar is dissolved, add the citrus juices and the orange rind. The sugar will caramelize as the juice hits it but it will liquify again later.

**3** Cook this for a while until the liquid thickens, and then place the bananas in it.

**4** Pour the arrack or brandy over the dish and set it aflame (if using red wine, this will not flame so just pour it over). Serve immediately with a sprinkling of cinnamon on top.

# koti ciri

makes **2** drinks

cheetah milk cocktail

| | |
|---|---|
| 1 egg yolk | 1 clove |
| 1/3 cup / 80 ml arrack or dark rum | 1/4 teaspoon grated nutmeg |
| 2 tablespoons sugar | 2/3 cup / 160 ml cold milk |
| zest of lime or lemon | |

**1** Put all the ingredients, except the milk, into a bowl or blender and whisk well.

**2** Then pour in the chilled milk; whisk again and serve immediately.

# rice & coconut pudding

serves **4**

½ cup / 110 g short grain rice, cooked

⅓ cup / 60 g sugar

½ cup / 30 g desiccated coconut

¼ cup / 60 ml coconut milk

½ teaspoon lemon rind, grated

¼ teaspoon cinnamon

salt

**1** Place the cooked rice in a pan and add the sugar, coconut, coconut milk and a pinch of salt. Mix well and cook very gently over a low heat, stirring frequently to prevent sticking.

**2** After 5 minutes or so, add the grated lemon rind and mix well. Transfer to a serving dish and sprinkle with cinnamon. Chill before serving.

# khao niaw ma maung

serves **4**

## rice dessert

**¹/₂ cup / 110 g short-grain rice, soaked**

**1 tablespoon coconut milk powder**

**seeds from 1 green cardamom pod, crushed**

**sugar**

**1 tablespoon dried/desiccated coconut, toasted**

**salt**

**FOR THE SYRUP\***

**¹/₂ cup / 120 ml water**

**¹/₂ cup / 110 g sugar**

\*You could use ready-made syrup or clear honey instead.

**1** Set a pan of water on to boil. Add the rice when it is boiling and cook for 10 minutes or so. Drain.

**2** Turn the rice into a bowl and put in the coconut milk powder, cardamom seeds and sugar.

**3** Add a pinch of salt and mix the ingredients well. Scatter the toasted coconut on top and serve as it is, or with syrup, below.

**4** To make the syrup, dissolve the sugar in the water as you bring it to the boil. Then hard boil for 10-15 minutes until it thickens. Pour over the individual portions and serve hot or cold.

# xoi nuoc dir a

serves **4**

coconut cream and rice dessert

1 cup / 200 g short-grain rice

thin coconut cream – 1 cup / 100 g creamed coconut mixed in 3 cups / 700 ml warm water

$1/_2$ cup / 120 ml coconut milk

salt

2 tablespoons brown sugar

$1/_2$ cup / 120 ml water

$1/_2$ teaspoon ground cinnamon

dash of vanilla essence

1 First, put the rice in a pan with the thin coconut cream and a little salt if desired. Cover the pot and cook over a moderate heat until it begins to boil. Then turn down the heat and simmer for about 10-20 minutes depending on the type of rice you are using. If using glutinous rice, it will form a thick paste.

2 Now spoon the rice into a greased 10 inch/25 cm baking tray. Cover it with foil, pierced in two places to let the steam escape. Set the tray over a pan of boiling water and steam it until the rice is firm. Put to one side to cool and then chill in the fridge.

3 Meanwhile, prepare a sauce by dissolving the sugar in the water. Bring to the boil and simmer without stirring until the mixture becomes slightly sticky. Add the cinnamon and vanilla and stir to mix them in. Now remove the sauce from the heat, let it cool and then chill it.

4 To serve, put the rice into individual bowls, then spoon on a little sauce and the coconut milk.

# latin
# america
# & caribbean

# corn/maize bread

| | |
|---|---|
| ¹/₂ cup / 70 g margarine, melted | 3 teaspoons baking powder |
| ¹/₂ cup / 110 g sugar | ¹/₂ teaspoon nutmeg |
| 1 egg, beaten | 1 cup / 240 ml milk |
| 1 cup / 125 g corn/maize meal | pinch of salt |
| 1 cup / 125 g flour | |

*Heat oven to*
*350°F/180°C/Gas 4*

**1** Mix the margarine and sugar together. Then add the egg and the corn/maize meal.

**2** Next sift in the flour and baking powder. Now add the nutmeg and salt and pour in the milk, stirring to mix well.

**3** When this is done, grease an 8 inch/20 cm square baking tin and spoon or pour the mixture into it. Bake for about 1 hour.

# limeade

makes **6-8** drinks

**5 limes or 3 lemons, unpeeled and roughly cut (remove pips)**

**sugar to taste**

**water to taste**

1 Put the lime or lemon chunks with the sugar and water into a blender and liquidize.

2 Strain, add ice and serve.

# pisara

serves **4**

quinoa dessert

**¹/₂ cup / 110 g quinoa,
toasted lightly**

**2¹/₂ cups / 590 ml water**

**sugar or honey to taste**

**1** Heat the water in a pan and when it is boiling put in the toasted quinoa. Cover the pan and simmer for about 15 minutes or until all the moisture is taken up.

**2** Stir in the sugar or honey to taste and serve at once.

# sweet potato pie

serves **4**

3 cups / 450 g sweet potatoes, cooked and mashed

1 medium can pineapple chunks, drained

1-2 tablespoons melted margarine

1 tablespoon brown sugar*

3 cloves, crushed or $^1/_2$ teaspoon ground cloves

$^1/_2$ tablespoon lemon juice

$^1/_2$ cup / 50 g breadcrumbs or toasted oats*

*optional ingredients

*Heat oven to 400°F/200°C/Gas 6*

**1** Mix all the ingredients
together in a bowl, saving a
few pieces of pineapple for
the topping.

**2** Now turn the mixture into
an ungreased dish or cake tin,
sprinkle on the breadcrumbs
and decorate with the pieces
of pineapple.

**3** Bake for about 30 minutes.
If using toasted oats, sprinkle
these on before serving.

CARIBBEAN

# banana bread

serves **6**

**3 large ripe bananas**

**³/₄ cup / 175 g margarine**

**1 cup / 175 g brown sugar**

**1³/₄ cups / 225 g flour**

**pinch of salt**

**¹/₂ teaspoon ground cinnamon***

**2 teaspoons baking powder**

**1 large egg**

**1 cup / 125 g walnuts, coarsely chopped**

**1 cup / 100 g raisins or sultanas***

*optional ingredient

*Heat oven to 350°F/180°C/Gas 4*

1 Peel the bananas and then mash them, using a large bowl. Then beat in the margarine. When this is combined, shake in the sugar and add the sieved flour, salt, cinnamon and baking powder. Mix this well with a wooden spoon.

2 Now crack the egg and blend it in before adding the chopped walnuts and raisins or sultanas.

3 Grease a 2 pound/1 kg bread or cake tin and spoon in the mixture.

4 Bake the bread for about $1^1/_2$ hours, and test for readiness by pushing a knife or skewer into the middle. It should come out cleanly if the bread is done.

5 Turn out onto a wire rack and leave it to cool completely before serving the cake.

# cassava cookies

| | |
|---|---|
| 2 pounds / 900 g cassava/manioc, peeled | 1 teaspoon baking powder |
| $^3/_4$ cup / 175 g margarine | 4 teaspoons ground cinnamon |
| 1 cup / 175 g brown sugar | 3 cups / 375 g flour |
| 2 eggs | |
| 3 cups / 225 g desiccated coconut | |

*Heat oven to
400°F/200°C/Gas 6*

**1** First grate the peeled cassava finely. Now place it in the center of a clean cloth or tea towel, draw up the corners and then twist and squeeze it to extract as much juice as possible.

**2** After this, take a large bowl and cream together the margarine and sugar. Then add the eggs, grated cassava and coconut and mix them well.

**3** Sieve in the baking powder, cinnamon and the flour, adding enough of this to make a stiff dough.

**4** Now take the dough from the bowl and knead it for at least 5 minutes.

**5** Roll it out on a floured surface to $1/2$ inch/1 cm thickness and cut into biscuit shapes with a cutter or into other shapes with a knife.

**6** Put the biscuits on baking sheets, about 2 inches/5 cm apart and bake them for 15-20 minutes until they are golden brown.

# ginger beer

makes approx. **1 quart/1 liter**

**1 large fresh ginger root, peeled and grated**

**4 sticks cinnamon**

**4 cloves**

**1¹/₂ cups / 260 g sugar**

**2 lemons or limes**

**4 cups / 940 ml water**

**1** Put the ginger into a pan and add the cinnamon, cloves, sugar, juice and zest/thinly pared skin of the lemons or limes. Pour in the water.

**2** Bring this to the boil, stirring all the time, and allow it to continue boiling for 10 minutes.

**3** When this is done, strain the liquid into a pitcher/jug and allow it to cool. Test the flavor, adding more water, lemon or lime juice, or sugar as required.

**4** Chill, and then serve with ice cubes and slices of lime or lemon on top.

# passion fruit/grenadillo juice

makes **1-2** drinks

**12 passion fruits/ grenadillos**

**1 cup / 240 ml water**

**juice of 2 lemons or limes**

**sugar to taste**

**1** Cut the passion fruits/grenadillos in half and scrape the pulp and seeds into a pan. Add the water and bring to simmering point.

**2** Cool and add the lemon juice and sugar. Chill before using.

serves **4**

# baked bananas with molasses

**4 bananas, halved lengthwise**

**$1/2$-1 tablespoon molasses or black treacle**

**juice of $1/2$ lime**

**$1/2$ teaspoon cinnamon**

**$1/2$ teaspoon allspice, ground**

**$1/2$ tablespoon grated orange rind**

**$1/2$ tablespoon sugar**

**a little margarine**

**1-2 tablespoons rum**

**1** Grease a shallow ovenproof dish with the margarine and lay the banana halves in it. Spoon the molasses over them.

**2** Combine the rest of the ingredients, except 1 tablespoon of the rum, in a small bowl and then pour the mixture over the bananas and molasses.

**3** Bake for 10-15 minutes and when ready to serve, heat the remaining rum in a spoon over a flame until it ignites. Then quickly pour it over the bananas and serve immediately.

*Heat oven to 350°F/180°C/Gas 4*

# CARIBBEAN

# rum punch

## with pineapple

2 tablespoons lime juice

1 tablespoon castor
sugar

$1/2$ teaspoon grated
nutmeg

4 tablespoons orange or
pineapple juice

dash of Angostura bitters*

2-4 tablespoons rum

*optional ingredient

**1** Put all ingredients into a blender and then serve over cracked ice.

CHILE

# manzanas asadas

serves **6**

baked apples

**6 large cooking apples, cored**

**4-6 tablespoons brown sugar**

**1¼ cups / 300 ml red wine or sherry**

**1 stick cinnamon**

**yogurt or cream***

*optional ingredient

*Heat oven to 400°F/200°C/Gas 6*

**1** Pierce the apple skins and then place them in a greased ovenproof dish. Pile the sugar into the hollows.

**2** Pour the wine or sherry into each apple, on and around them. Add the cinnamon stick and then put the dish into the oven for about 20-30 minutes until the apples are cooked. Serve with yogurt or cream.

# pineapple daiquiri

serves **2**

**1 cup / 240 ml pineapple juice**

**1 tablespoon orange liqueur**

**$1/2$ cup / 120 ml light rum**

**juice of $1/2$ lime**

**sugar to taste**

**ice cubes**

**1** Place everything except the ice into a blender or beat well with a whisk.

**2** Now put the ice cubes in a clean cloth and whack them with a rolling pin or hammer to crush the ice.

**3** Heap the cracked ice into the glasses and pour the daiquiri over.

# banana, rum & orange cocktail

serves **2**

1 banana, peeled
and chopped

juice of 3 oranges or 1
cup / 240 ml orange juice

3 tablespoons rum

cracked ice

**1** Mix the banana and orange juice together in a blender or beat with a whisk. Add the rum and pour over the cracked ice in a glass.

# baked bananas

serves **4**

4 large bananas

1 tablespoon margarine

2 tablespoons honey

juice of 1 lemon

small carton soured cream or plain yogurt

1 cup / 125 g nuts (cashews or walnuts or a mixture of both)*

¹/₂ cup / 100 g raisins or sultanas*

*optional ingredient

*Heat oven to 350°F/180°C/Gas 4*

**1** Peel the bananas and cut them in half, lengthwise. Place them in a greased baking dish and dot with the margarine.

**2** Then mix the honey and lemon juice together and spread this over the bananas. Put the dish in the oven and bake for 10-20 minutes. Serve hot with soured cream or yogurt and nuts and dried fruit.

GUYANA

# rum swizzle

makes **2** glasses

**1 tablespoon castor sugar**

**2-4 tablespoons lime juice**

**2 sprigs mint**

**1/2 teaspoon cinnamon**

**3 tablespoons rum**

1 Put everything, except one of the sprigs of mint, into a jug and stir until the mixture is frothy (or use a blender). Pour onto cracked ice and decorate with remaining mint.

# sweet potato cake

serves **4**

**¹/₂ pound / 225 g sweet potato, chopped into small cubes**

**¹/₂ cup / 120 ml milk**

**2 bananas, mashed**

**¹/₂ teaspoon cinnamon**

**2 tablespoons sugar**

**2 egg yolks, beaten**

**1 cup / 100 g raisins or sultanas**

**1 tablespoon rum***

**a little margarine**

*optional ingredient

*Heat oven to 300°F/150°C/Gas 2*

**1** First, cook the sweet potato pieces in boiling water for 20 minutes or until soft. Drain thoroughly.

**2** Now put back into the saucepan and mash with a fork. Add the milk and blend well. Then add the bananas and stir in the cinnamon, sugar, egg yolks, raisins or sultanas and rum.

**3** Mix all the ingredients well and then spoon the mixture into a greased oven dish. Bake for 45 minutes or until firm to the touch and golden on top. Serve from the dish, hot, accompanied with cream or yogurt.

# HONDURAS

# dulce de leche

milk dessert

| | |
|---|---|
| 3 cups / 700 ml milk | **1** Pour the milk into a heavy saucepan and add the sugar, ground almonds and cinnamon. Bring to boiling point. |
| 1/2 cup / 110 g sugar | |
| 2 tablespoons ground almonds | |
| 1 stick cinnamon | **2** Cook over a medium heat, stirring all the time, for half an hour or so until the mixture thickens. Remove the stick of cinnamon before serving either warm or cold. |

# gingerbread serves 6

1 cup / 125 g
self-raising flour

<sup>1</sup>/<sub>2</sub> teaspoon
ground allspice

1-2 teaspoons ground
ginger

<sup>1</sup>/<sub>3</sub> cup / 60 g sugar

1 tablespoon molasses or
black treacle

<sup>1</sup>/<sub>2</sub> cup / 100 g butter or
margarine

1 tablespoon raisins
or sultanas

1 tablespoon milk

1 tablespoon rum

1 egg, beaten

*Heat oven to
350°F/180°C/Gas 4*

1 First, sift the flour into a bowl and add the allspice, ginger and raisins or sultanas.

2 Now melt the margarine or butter and put in the sugar and molasses or black treacle. Mix well.

3 When that is done pour the milk into the beaten egg and stir together. Then combine this with the melted butter mixture.

4 Next, pour this into the flour, stirring carefully to integrate the ingredients.

5 Add the rum now and mix well. Spoon the mixture into a greased 8 x 4 inch/20 x 10 cm bread tin and bake for 45-60 minutes or until a skewer comes out cleanly. Leave in the tin for 15 minutes and then turn out onto a wire rack to cool.

# arroz de leche

serves **4-5**

rice pudding

| | |
|---|---|
| 1 cup / 240 ml water | 2 egg yolks, beaten |
| rind of 1 lemon, grated | $1/2$ cup / 50 g sultanas or raisins |
| $1/2$ cup / 110 g rice | 1 tablespoon margarine |
| 1 quart / 1 liter milk | $1/4$ teaspoon cinnamon |
| 1 stick cinnamon | salt |
| $1/2$ cup / 110 g sugar | |

1 Boil the cup of water together with the lemon rind and a little salt; put in the rice and cook until the water is absorbed and the rice is fluffy.

2 When this is done pour in the milk, add the stick of cinnamon and simmer gently for 10-15 minutes. Now put in the sugar and cook slowly for a further 10 minutes.

3 Remove the pan from the heat and add the egg yolks and sultanas or raisins, stirring as you do this.

4 When these ingredients have amalgamated, bring the saucepan back to the heat and bring the mixture just to boiling point.

5 Cook gently, stirring all the time, for 5 minutes more or until the mixture has the consistency of a custard. Put in the margarine and sprinkle the cinnamon over the top just before serving. Serve hot or cool.

# fresh fruit salad

serves **4**

**2 mangoes**

**4 peaches**

**6 plums**

**1 cup / 100 g cherries, stoned**

**1 cup / 100 g strawberries**

**cream or yogurt***

*optional ingredient

1 Wash and cut up the fruit into small pieces and serve with cream or yogurt if liked.

# middle east & north africa

# walnut & pumpkin pudding

serves **4**

¹/₂ cup / 110 g sugar

¹/₂ cup / 120 ml water

1 pound / 450 g pumpkin, cubed

¹/₃ cup / 30 g walnuts, chopped

1 tablespoon lemon juice

1 cup / 225 g cream or yogurt*

*optional ingredient

**1** To begin, make a syrup by dissolving the sugar in the water over a gentle heat. Then increase the temperature and boil hard for 5-10 minutes, stirring continuously, until the mixture thickens but does not yet caramelize.

**2** Put the pumpkin cubes into the syrup and cook gently with the lid on for 1 minute. Then remove the cover and continue to simmer, turning from time to time until the pumpkin is cooked and has absorbed almost all the syrup.

**3** Mix in the walnuts and then transfer the pumpkin to a serving dish and sprinkle the lemon juice over. Serve hot or cold with the cream or yogurt.

JORDAN

# mugle

serves **4**

spiced rice dessert

**1/2 cup / 60 g rice flour**

**1/4 teaspoon ground cinnamon**

**1/4 teaspoon ground caraway**

**1/4 teaspoon ground aniseed**

**1-2 tablespoons sugar**

**2 cups / 480 ml water**

**1/2 cup / 65 g walnuts or almonds, chopped, or pine nuts**

**a few drops of orange water***

*optional Ingredient available from Indian stores.

**1** Place the rice flour in a saucepan with the cinnamon, caraway and aniseed. Mix well and then gradually pour in the water, stirring all the time.

**2** Bring slowly to the boil, then cook rapidly for 2 minutes, stirring continuously as the mixture thickens.

**3** Now put in the sugar and boil for 2-3 minutes. Allow to cool a little, add the orange water and then pour into serving bowls. Decorate with the nuts and accompany with cream or yogurt.

# fruit salad

serves **4-6**

**1-2 tablespoons
clear honey**

**2 tablespoons mulberry
or orange syrup, van der
hum, kirsch or cointreau**

**1 cup / 240 ml cold tea**

**$^1/_2$ cup / 120 ml
orange juice**

**2 tablespoons rose water**

**8 dried figs, cut into
$^1/_2$ inch / 1.5 cm pieces**

**10-15 dried dates,
stoned and halved**

**2 tablespoons sultanas
or raisins**

**2 tablespoons whole
hazelnuts**

**1 tablespoon whole
almonds**

**2 tablespoons pistachio
or cashew nuts**

**1 small melon or 2
peaches**

**1 orange, peeled and
chopped**

1 Start by mixing the honey with the syrup or liqueur and blend in the cold tea, orange juice and rose water.

2 Now add the figs, dates, sultanas or raisins, hazelnuts, almonds and 1 tablespoon of the pistachio or cashew nuts. When these have combined well, put the bowl into the refrigerator and leave for 2 hours to soak.

3 After this, slice open the melon and discard the seeds. Cut the fruit into slices and then remove as much of the flesh as possible by dicing into cubes or small pieces. Add the melon (or peaches if using) and the orange to the bowl of fruit and nuts and mix well. Return the fruit salad to the refrigerator for another hour.

4 Chop the remaining pistachio or cashew nuts and scatter them over the salad before serving with yogurt or cream.

# halwa ditzmar

makes **15**

date slices

| |
|---|
| **¹/₂ pound / 225 g dates, stoned and chopped finely** |
| **¹/₄ pound / 110 g figs, chopped finely** |
| **1 cup / 110 g walnuts, ground coarsely** |
| **¹/₄ teaspoon aniseed** |
| **¹/₄ teaspoon ground coriander** |
| **2 teaspoons clear honey** |
| **a few drops orange water\*** |

**\*optional ingredient**

1 Put the chopped dates and figs into a bowl and stir in the ground walnuts. Mix well and then add the aniseed and coriander, the orange water if using and the honey.

2 Then press the mixture into a 6 inch / 15 cm cake tin. Chill for 2 hours and then serve cut into small squares. It will store for one week.

# khoshaf

serves **4**

dried fruit salad

**1 cup / 100 g dried apricots**

**1 cup / 100 g dried prunes**

**1 cup / 100 g dried figs or dates**

**1/2 cup / 50 g raisins or sultanas**

**1/2 cup / 60 g almonds or pinenuts/pignoles**

**1/2 cup / 120 ml cold tea**

**1 cup / 240 ml orange juice**

1 Soak the fruit for 1 hour in the tea and orange juice (the liquid should just cover the fruit. Add more or less as required).

2 To serve, place the softened fruit and liquid into a bowl and sprinkle the nuts over. Then you can either serve it as it is, cold, or put it into a gentle oven for 20-30 minutes and serve warm.

# apple & almond dessert

serves **4**

4 large cooking apples, peeled, cored and chopped

a little water

1 tablespoon brown sugar, or to taste

$^1/_4$ cup / 50 g ground almonds

$^1/_4$ cup / 25 g raisins or sultanas, soaked in water for one hour

$^1/_2$ cup / 50 g dried apricots, soaked in water for one hour and chopped into small pieces

$^1/_2$ cup / 60 g whole almonds

*Heat oven to 325°F/160°C/Gas 3 – if serving hot: see point 4.*

**1** First of all, put the apples into a saucepan with a little water. Bring to the boil and then reduce the heat and simmer until the apples are very soft. Some varieties of apple will purée themselves while cooking and this is fine for this dish.

**2** Next mash the apples with a spoon adding sugar as required. Then add the ground almonds and mix well.

**3** Scatter the raisins or sultanas, apricots and whole almonds over the surface.

**4** Put into the oven for 10 minutes, or serve warm as it is. The dish can also be chilled and served cold.

serves **2-4**

# halva

## with almonds

**¹/₂ cup / 85 g sugar**

**1¹/₄ cups / 300 ml water**

**8 tablespoons / 100 g margarine**

**¹/₂ cup / 125 g semolina**

**¹/₂ cup / 50 g raisins**

**¹/₂ cup / 60 g almonds, chopped**

**¹/₂ teaspoon ground cinnamon**

**seeds from 1 cardamom pod, crushed**

**1** Cook the sugar and water together over a medium heat until they make a thick syrup.

**2** In another pan, melt the margarine and brown the semolina in it. Then put in the raisins, almonds, cinnamon and cardamom and stir well.

**3** Now pour the syrup into the pan containing the semolina mix, stir it in and let it simmer for 3-4 minutes. Spoon or pour the dessert into a bowl and serve either hot or cold.

makes **1** cup

# ayran

yogurt drink

½ cup / 110 g yogurt

½ cup / 120 ml water or
⅔ cup / 160 ml milk

pinch of dried mint

salt

1 Put the yogurt into a bowl and slowly pour in the water or milk, beating as you do so; or blend the ingredients.

2 Then add the mint and salt, mix well. Refrigerate before you serve the drink.

# almond crescents

makes approx. **20**

**1¹/₂ cups / 110 g ground almonds**

**1/₂ pound / 225 g margarine**

**2 tablespoons icing sugar**

**1 egg yolk**

**1 tablespoon brandy***

**2 cups / 250 g flour**

**1/₂ teaspoon baking powder**

**1 tablespoon sesame seeds**

**a few drops of almond essence**

*Or use 1/₂ teaspoon vanilla essence.

*Heat oven to 325°F/160°C/Gas 3*

**1** Start by roasting the ground almonds on a baking sheet in the oven for about 10 minutes or until they turn a deeper golden shade.

**2** Cream the margarine in a bowl and then add the 2 tablespoons of icing sugar and the egg yolk. Mix well before adding the brandy or vanilla essence and the ground almonds.

**3** Sift the flour and baking powder into the almond mixture, combining ingredients with a wooden spoon.

**4** Take up walnut-sized pieces of dough and form into crescent shapes. Press a few sesame seeds on top and then place them on a baking sheet and cook for about 30 minutes or until very lightly browned.

**5** Remove from the oven and leave to cool for a few minutes. Sift a little icing sugar over and then leave to cool completely before eating.

# spiced tea

serves **4**

tea leaves or tea bags for 4

1 teaspoon fresh ginger, chopped

2 cloves

1 stick cinnamon

1 teaspoon ground coriander

1 tablespoon aniseed

4 whole almonds

**1** Pour enough water for 4 cups of tea into a pan together with the ingredients.

**2** Bring to the boil and simmer gently for 5-10 minutes or until the water is dark. Add honey if desired.

# muhallabia

serves **2-4**

## rice and almond dessert

**¹/₄ cup / 50 g ground rice**

**2¹/₂ cups / 590 ml milk**

**2 tablespoons rose water
or orange blossom water**

**¹/₄ cup / 50 g sugar**

**¹/₄ cup / 50 g ground
almonds**

**¹/₂ tablespoon almonds,
sliced lengthwise**

**¹/₂ tablespoon unsalted,
shelled pistachios,
chopped**

**1** Put the ground rice into a large bowl and gradually pour in about half a cup/120 ml of the milk, stirring all the time to make a smooth paste.

**2** Now bring the rest of the milk to boiling point in a saucepan. Then blend it into the rice mixture, stirring thoroughly so that it remains smooth.

**3** After that, pour the mixture back into the pan. Heat and stir until it begins to boil and thicken.

**4** Now spoon in the orange blossom water or rose water and cook for a further minute, before adding the ground almonds. Stir and mix well and then pour into a serving dish. Decorate with the sliced almonds and pistachios and chill before eating.

# fresh orange dessert

serves **4-6**

**6 oranges, peeled**

**$1/2$-1 teaspoon ground cinnamon**

**2 teaspoons orange blossom water**

**icing sugar***

*optional ingredient

1 Remove any pith from the oranges and slice them into thin rounds. Lay them on a flat plate and sprinkle on the icing sugar, cinnamon and orange blossom water.

2 Place in the refrigerator for 1 hour, but turn the slices over from time to time during that period. Serve with cinnamon biscuits.

# cinnamon cookies

2 cups / 250 g flour
1/2 cup / 120 ml oil
1 cup / 225 g sugar
rind of 1 lemon, grated
ground cinnamon

*Heat oven to
350°F/180°C/Gas 4*

1 To begin, grease and flour a baking sheet. Next sift the flour into a large bowl and then make a well in the center and pour in the oil. Add the sugar and lemon rind and mix well to form a dough.

2 Now take small balls of the dough and shape them into little flat round cookies. Place them on the baking sheet and sprinkle some cinnamon on top.

3 Bake for 20 minutes and then let them cool a little before eating.

# samsa

makes approx **20**

## almond pastries

| | |
|---|---|
| **¹/₂ pound / 225 g ground almonds** | **FOR THE SYRUP** |
| **¹/₂ cup / 110 g sugar** | **juice of 1 lemon or lime** |
| **2 teaspoons grated orange peel** | **2 tablespoons geranium or rose water\*** |
| **2 teaspoons ground cinnamon** | **1 cup / 225 g castor sugar** |
| **¹/₂ pound / 225 g filo pastry** | **1¹/₄ cups / 300 ml water** |
| **¹/₄ pound / 110 g margarine, melted** | **1 tablespoon sesame seeds, toasted+** |

*Available in specialist and oriental grocery stores.

+To toast the sesame seeds, place them under the grill or broiler for a few minutes, shaking the tray frequently. They will turn a deeper shade.

*Heat oven to 350°F/180°C/Gas 4*

**1** Place the ground almonds in a bowl and add the sugar, orange peel and cinnamon and combine well.

**2** Grease a baking sheet and then cut filo pastry sheets into rectangles measuring 6 x 10 inches/15 x 25 cm, or cut them as required. Keep the remainder covered so that they do not become brittle. Brush each sheet with melted margarine as you use it.

**3** Place a tablespoonful of the almond mixture on the end of the pastry strip. Next, fold the long sides inwards and then roll up the pastry into a cigar shape.

**4** When this is done, arrange the cakes, seam side down, on the greased baking sheet and cook in the oven for 15-20 minutes until they are golden.

**5** While they are baking, heat the water together with the rest of the sugar and cook, stirring until the sugar dissolves. Then add the lemon or lime juice.

**6** Bring to the boil, stirring constantly, and hard boil for 15-20 minutes until the mixture thickens to make a syrup that coats the back of a spoon. Then sprinkle in the geranium or rose water and set aside.

**7** When the pastries are baked, let them cool a little on a wire tray and then arrange them on a plate and pour the syrup over. Scatter the sesame seeds on top.

SYRIA

# ma'mounia

serves **4**

## semolina halva dessert

**1 tablespoon margarine**

**1 cup / 150 g semolina**

**2¹/₂ cups / 590 ml milk
(or half milk, half water)**

**¹/₂ cup / 110 g sugar**

**1 teaspoon ground
cinnamon**

**1 tablespoon
pignoles/pine nuts***

*optional ingredient

**1** Heat the margarine in a saucepan and add the semolina. Cook it gently and stir it round for about 5 minutes until it deepens in color.

**2** In a separate pan, bring the milk or milk and water to the boil with the sugar and then pour this gradually over the semolina. Stir over a low heat and cook until the mixture thickens.

**3** When it is ready, set the pan aside, covered, for 15 minutes. Then serve it, cool, with cinnamon and the pignoles/pine nuts on top.

# kibrizli cake

serves **6-8**

semolina cake

| | |
|---|---|
| ¹/₂ cup/125 g semolina | ²/₃ cup / 150 ml water |
| 5 eggs | a little salt* |
| ³/₄ cup / 130 g sugar | 1 tablespoon sesame seeds |
| grated rind and juice of 1 lemon | 2 tablespoons honey |
| ¹/₂ cup / 125 g ground almonds | *optional ingredient |
| ¹/₄ teaspoon baking powder | |

*Heat oven to 350°F/180°C/Gas 4*

**1** First, lightly grease a deep 8 inch/20 cm cake tin and line it with greaseproof paper.

**2** Now crack the eggs and separate the whites into a large bowl, putting the yolks in another.

**3** Add the sugar and lemon rind (save the juice for the glaze, see 7) to the egg yolks and beat them together until the mixture is a pale color.

**4** Now put in the semolina, ground almonds, baking powder and water and mix till smooth.

**5** Add the salt to the egg whites and whisk them till they are becoming firm. Then, using a metal spoon, fold them into yolk mixture and pour this into the cake tin.

**6** Sprinkle the sesame seeds on top and bake the cake in the center of the oven for about 40-45 minutes until the cake is firm to the touch.

**7** Just before the cake is cooked, warm the honey in a small saucepan and then boil it hard for 4 minutes. Remove from the heat and stir in the lemon juice.

**8** When the cake is ready, spoon the warm syrup over it while it is still hot and in the tin. Allow the cake to cool and then loosen it carefully before turning out.

# nutrition facts

**With increasing concern** about obesity in the West, and poor nutrition in many Majority World countries, it is useful to know what we require from our food – and what we do not need. Buying fair trade and organic produce improves the quality of what we eat while also supporting ethical farming and trading practices.

Humans need carbohydrates, fiber, protein, fat, vitamins and minerals as well as water. These maintain our bodies and give us energy, measured in calories. A person's calorie requirement varies according to their age, health, size and activity level. A small person with a sedentary life may only require 2,000 calories a day, while someone who is large and does heavy physical work may need 3,500. The UN agencies recommend a minimum daily intake (RDI) for adults of 2,300-2,600 calories per person.

Ideally, calories should be drawn from the range of nutrients listed above. The main or macro-nutrients – carbohydrates, protein and fat – provide different amounts of calories. Fat is very high in calories: one gram of oil, butter or margarine supplies nine calories. Carbohydrates (from sugars and starches) and protein (from beans, nuts and dairy foods) provide four calories for each gram. Alcohol delivers seven calories per gram (or milliliter), so a glass of dry white wine would be about 100 calories.

## Protein
Protein is the body's building material. It is made up of amino acids; foods contain these in differing proportions. The highest-quality protein foods contain the most complete set of essential amino acids in the right proportions for the body to be able to

make the best use of them. According to the American Dietetics Association, 'plant sources of protein alone can provide adequate amounts of essential amino acids if a variety of plant foods are consumed and energy needs are met.' The UN Food and Agriculture Organization recommends that around 10 per cent of a person's energy intake should come from protein. So on the 2,600 RDI calories about 260 should be from protein. Since each gram of protein provides four calories, you would therefore need 65 grams of protein each day, depending on your age, sex, lifestyle and so on. The UN figure leaves a comfortable margin: the Vegetarian Society in Britain suggests that 45 grams per day is plenty for women (more if pregnant, breastfeeding or very active) and 55 grams for men (more if very active).

People in the rich world rarely lack protein because overall we consume well above the 2,600 calories level and within that food intake there is likely to be sufficient protein. It is a different situation in countries where the overall calorie consumption is low (the 500 million people of the least developed countries rarely consume more than 2,000 calories; one of the lowest national averages is Sierra Leone's 1,880).

Vegetarian foods rich in protein include nuts, seeds, pulses (peas, beans, lentils), grains, dairy produce, eggs and soy products such as tofu. Vegetables, salads and fruit contribute small amounts of amino acids as well.

**Carbohydrates**
Carbohydrates are the main source of energy. In plant foods, these normally come as sugars and starches. Avoid sugars and refined starches (white bread, white rice) as although they bring

calories, they bring few nutrients. By contrast, cereals such as wholemeal bread, pasta, oats and root vegetables like potatoes and parsnips, bring nourishment along with the same amount of calories. They also provide fiber or roughage.

### Fats and oils

In the West we consume a lot of energy as fat and sugar, in processed and fast foods (cakes, biscuits, ice-cream, chips and pies). This can result in heart disease and obesity, illnesses which kill around 2.5 million people each year.

A little fat is essential to keep body tissues healthy, for the manufacture of hormones and to carry the vitamins A, D, E and K. Fats are made up of fatty acids. There are saturated and unsaturated fats, referring to how much hydrogen they contain.

Saturated fats, found mainly in animal products, contain cholesterol. Our bodies need this but can produce what they require. Excess cholesterol can clog arteries, leading to increased risk of heart disease. Saturated fats raise blood cholesterol levels while unsaturated fats – such as olive and sunflower oil – lower them.

WHO advises between 15-30 per cent of total energy intake as fat, with no more than 10 per cent of it in the form of saturated fat. So if your calorie intake is 2,600, and 20 per cent of this comes from fat, that would give 520 calories. Since each gram of fat brings nine calories, this means you should eat about 58 g or two ounces a day.  The West's daily average is double that, contributing 1,080 calories before adding those from protein and carbohydrates.

Dairy products are laden with saturated fat, especially hard cheeses, cream and whole milk. Choose low-fat yogurt, cottage or low-fat cheese and skimmed milk that also deliver useful protein. Plant foods rich in fats – avocado pears, nuts and seeds – should be eaten in moderation. Unlike crisps or French fries, however, nuts and seeds do also provide protein, vitamins and a substantial amount of fiber. Pulses, whole grains, vegetables and fruit are low in fat.

## Vitamins
These are nutrients that the body cannot produce for itself either at all or in sufficient quantities. Vitamins are essential for growth, cell repair and regulating metabolism (the rate at which the body consumes energy). Green leafy vegetables are a major source of many vitamins and minerals – try to eat them uncooked when you can.

## Minerals
These keep the body functioning properly. Calcium, iron, potassium and magnesium are the main minerals; others such as zinc and iodine are known as trace elements and are needed only in tiny amounts. ■

# fair trade food

**Fairly traded (and organic)** products are becoming widely available. If you can't find them where you shop, keep asking. Even giant supermarkets have to listen to their customers. They have huge power over producers; this is part of the problem with 'free' trade. So shopping in smaller stores, or through aid organizations, is a good way to support fair trade. The products cost a little more, because fair trade producers are paid above the cost of production.

The price of almost all food commodities from the South has been falling to below production cost, thus impoverishing farmers while traders and retailers have prospered.

## Where to buy?
Fair trade food products are available from alternative outlets, see below.

## The International Federation for Alternative Trade (IFAT)
A network of fair trade organizations, many of them Southern producers. They have agreed common objectives:
● To improve the livelihoods of producers ● To promote development opportunities for disadvantaged producers ● To raise consumer awareness ● To set an example of partnership in trade ● To campaign for changes in conventional trade ● To protect human rights.
**www.ifat.org**

IFAT members who sell some of the food products for the recipes in this book:
**Australia**
Community Aid Abroad Trading:
www.caatrading.org.au
**Britain**
Traidcraft Exchange:
www.traidcraft.co.uk

**Canada**
Level Ground Trading Ltd:
www.levelground.com
**Japan**
Global Village Fair Trade
Company:
www.globalvillage.org.jp

**New Zealand/Aotearoa**
Trade Aid Importers Ltd:
www.tradeaid.org.nz
**US**
Equal Exchange:
www.equalexchange.com

---

**Fair Trade Labelling Organizations International (FLO)**
Most national fair trade labels are now members of FLO. Their common principles include:
• Democratic organization of production • Unrestricted access to free trade unions • No child labor • Decent working conditions • A price that covers the costs of production • Long-term relationships • A social premium to improve conditions • Environmental sustainability

The FLO monitoring program ensures that the trading partners comply with fair trade criteria and that individual producers benefit.

Most national fair trade labels adopt the main elements of a common logo (left). **www.fairtrade.net**

**Britain**
The Fairtrade Foundation:
www.fairtrade.org.uk
**Canada**
TransFair:
www.web.net/fairtrade
**Europe**
Max Havelaar:
www.maxhavelaar.nl
TransFair: www.transfair.org
**Ireland**
Fairtrade Mark Ireland:
www.fair-mark.org
**US**
TransFair:
www.transfairusa.org
**Japan**
TransFair:
www.transfair-jp.com

# index

*aam ras*                58
ALMONDS        46, 52, 60, 136, 138,
                  142, 144, 146
  ground        48, 68, 124, 144, 150,
                  154, 160
ANGOSTURA BITTERS        110
APPLE        22, 64, 112, 144
APRICOT, DRIED        142, 144
ARRACK        80, 82
*arroz de leche*        128
*ayran*        148

BANANA        14, 16, 22, 48, 64, 66, 72,
          80, 100, 108, 116, 118, 122
**biscuits**        102, 150, 158
BRANDY        26, 80
**breads**        10, 14, 18, 92, 100, 126
*bubor chacha*        70

**cakes**        30, 40, 60, 74, 122, 164
CARDAMOM PODS        48, 52, 56, 58,
                  62, 68, 146
CARROT        62
CASHEWS        60, 118, 138
CASSAVA (MANIOC)        102
CHERRIES        130
  glacé        60
*Christmas cake*        60
CINNAMON        68, 112, 146, 158
COCONUT
  creamed        40, 78, 88
  desiccated        30, 38, 42, 50, 84, 102
  milk        42, 64, 70, 76, 84, 88
CORN (MAIZE; SWEETCORN) MEAL
                  18, 92
CREAM        20, 62, 64
single        58

CURRANTS        60

*daiquiri, pineapple*        114
DATES        138, 140, 142
*docono*        16
**drinks**
  cold        54, 76, 82, 94, 104, 106, 110,
                  114, 116, 120, 148
  hot, see teas
*dulce de leche*        124

EGG        60

fair trade        170-1
FIG        138, 140
dried        142
FILO PASTRY        160
FLOUR
  rice        38, 136
  soy        12
  wheat        12
food facts        166-9
**fools**        20
**fruit salads**        22, 64, 130, 138, 142
**fudge**        48
*ful-sudani*        34

GINGER        68, 104, 126, 152
GRENADILLO (PASSION FRUIT)        22,
                  76, 106

*halva*        62, 146, 162
*halwa ditzmar*        140
HAZELNUTS        138
HONEY        26, 28
*hsing jen cha*        46

**ice-creams** 52

KEWRA WATER 70
*khao niaw ma maung* 86
*khoshaf* 142
*kibrizli cake* 164
*koti ciri* 82
*kulfi* 52

*lassi* 54
LEMON 94, 104, 106
LIME/JUICE 94, 104, 106, 108, 110, 114, 120
LYCHEE 64

**macaroons** 34
MAIZE *see* CORN
*mal pua* 38
*ma'mounia* 162
MANGO 20, 22, 58, 64, 130
MANIOC *see* CASSAVA
*manzanas asadas* 112
*mbatata pudding* 26
*melktart* 32
MELON 64, 138
*meni-meniyong* 28
MILK 32, 52, 78, 82, 124, 128, 148, 154, 162
evaporated 50
MINT 120, 148
MOLASSES 78, 126
*mugle* 136
*muhallabia* 154

NUTMEG 30, 110
NUTS *see* ALMONDS; CASHEWS;
  HAZELNUTS; PEANUTS;
  PINENUTS; PISTACHIOS; WALNUTS

ORANGE/JUICE 22, 76, 110, 116, 138, 156
ORANGE LIQUEUR 114

**pancakes** 38, 72
PAPAYA (PAWPAW) 20, 22, 64
PASSION FRUIT *see* GRENADILLO
**pastries** 160
PASTRY 32; *see also* FILO PASTRY
PAWPAW *see* PAPAYA
PEACH 130, 138
PEANUTS 10, 34, 44
PEAR 22
**pies** 98
PIGNOLES *see* PINE NUTS
PINE NUTS (PIGNOLES) 136, 142, 162
PINEAPPLE/JUICE 22, 64, 98, 110, 114
*pisang pancakes* 72
*pisara* 96
PISTACHIOS 46, 52, 62, 138, 154
PLUMS 130
PRUNES, DRIED 142
**puddings** 84, 134
PUMPKIN 134

QUINOA 96

RAISINS 60, 100, 122, 126, 128, 138, 142, 144, 146
RICE 128
  ground 154
  pudding 46
  short-grain 84, 86, 88

RUM        64, 74, 76, 82, 108, 110, 114, 116, 120, 126

SAFFRON    58, 68
*samsa*    160
**sauces**    66
**scones**    12
SEMOLINA   16, 40, 42, 146, 162, 164
SESAME SEEDS    28, 44, 160
SHERRY    26, 112
STRAWBERRIES    76, 130
SUGAR, BROWN    112
SULTANAS   60, 100, 122, 126, 128, 138, 142, 144
SWEETCORN *see* CORN
SWEET POTATO    26, 70, 98, 122
**syrups**    38, 86, 160

**tarts**    32
**teas**    56, 68, 152
TREACLE, BLACK    108, 126

*vattalappam*    78

WALNUTS   62, 100, 118, 134, 136, 140
WATERMELON    64
WINE, RED    80, 112

*xoi nuoc dir a*    88

YOGURT    54, 62, 148

ZALAK    64

# about the new internationalist

**www.newint.org**

**New Internationalist Publications** is a co-operative with offices in Oxford (England), Adelaide (Australia), Toronto (Canada) and Christchurch (New Zealand/Aotearoa). The monthly **New Internationalist** magazine now has more than 75,000 subscribers worldwide. In addition to the magazine and the **One World Almanac**, the co-operative also publishes the **One World Calendar**, an outstanding collection of full-colour photographs. It also publishes books, including: the successful series of **No-Nonsense Guides** to the key issues in the world today; cookbooks containing recipes and cultural information from around the world; and photographic books on topics such as Nomadic Peoples and Water. The **NI** is the English-language publisher of the biennial reference book **The World Guide**, written by the Instituto del Tercer Mundo in Uruguay.

The co-operative is financially independent but aims to break even; any surpluses are reinvested so as to bring **New Internationalist** publications to as many people as possible.

> 'The **New Internationalist** magazine is independent, lively and properly provocative, helping keep abreast of important developments in parts of our globe that risk marginalization. Read it!' – *ARCHBISHOP DESMOND TUTU, Cape Town, South Africa.*